T5-CCV-623

CONTENTS

The Heart's Song

Reflections on Love

THE HEART'S SONG

Reflections on Love

ARIEL BOOKS

ANDREWS AND McMEEL

KANSAS CITY

ISBN: 0-8362-0718-1

First Printing, July 1995
Second Printing, November 1996

Library of Congress Catalog Card Number: 95-76431

*I*NTRODUCTION

*P*OETS, NOVELISTS, AND PHILOSOPHERS HAVE ENDEAVORED to describe love for centuries. In this inspiring collection, the young, the old, the novice, and the veteran all have their say about this powerful emotion. According to Plato, "At the touch of love, everyone becomes a poet," and, indeed, love has a transforming effect on our lives.

Love affords the ordinary person a touch of eternity. "To love is to receive a glimpse of heaven," says Karen Sunde. When we love someone, we become part of the timeless energy of the universe that links us to all those who have loved before. We are connected to the force of life, and because love transcends all and conquers all, we feel initiated into the realm of the divine.

According to the French writer Molière, "The heart can do anything." Often, when we love someone—whether a spouse, a child, a friend, or a lover—we feel the truth of Molière's statement. Love gives us the strength to do things we ordinarily might not think we can do. How often do we feel the paradox of our heart expanding when we're pouring love out to others? "Nobody has ever measured, not even poets, how much the heart can hold," Zelda Fitzgerald aptly states.

Love can be difficult to find. Sometimes it skirts our lives with the elusiveness of a unicorn, and, often,—like a stubborn child—it won't come the first time we call. Usually, love can be found wherever kindness, respect, laughter, compassion, and genuine concern for other people abound. But however and wherever it appears, love changes our life forever As David Viscott says, "To love and be loved is to feel the sun from both sides."

Part I: Romantic Love

He gave her a look you could have poured on a waffle.

Ring Lardner

I loved Kirk so much,
I would have skied down
Mount Everest in the nude
with a carnation up my nose.

JOYCE McKINNEY

The heart that loves is always young.

GREEK PROVERB

I can see from your
utter misery, from your eagerness
to misunderstand each other,
and from your thoroughly bad temper,
that this is the real thing.

~ *Peter Ustinov* ~

Love is a fire. But whether it is going to warm your hearth or burn down your house, you can never tell.

JOAN CRAWFORD

I wouldn't give up one minute of
my time with Richard Burton . . .
We were like magnets,
alternating pulling towards each other
and inexorably pushing away.

— *Elizabeth Taylor* —

*Love sets you going like a
fat gold watch.*

SYLVIA PLATH

To love one who loves you,

to admire one who admires you,

in a word, to be the idol of one's idol,

is exceeding the limit of human joy;

it is stealing fire from heaven.

Delphine de Girardin

Whenas in silks my Julia goes,

Then, then (methinks) how sweetly flows

That liquefaction of her clothes.

Next, when I cast mine eyes and see

That brave vibration each way free;

Oh how that glittering taketh me!

Robert Herrick

I do love nothing in the world so well as you; is not that strange?

WILLIAM SHAKESPEARE

In my Sunday School class there was a beautiful little girl with golden curls. I was smitten at once and still am.

HARRY S. TRUMAN

(on his wife, Bess)

*People who throw kisses are
hopelessly lazy.*

— ~ —

BOB HOPE

Was this the face that

launched a thousand ships,

And burnt the topless towers of Ilium?

Sweet Helen,

make me immortal with a kiss.

Her lips suck forth my soul;

see, where it flies!

Christopher Marlowe

We can perhaps learn
to prepare for love. We can welcome
its coming, we can learn to treasure
and cherish it when it comes,
but we cannot make it happen.
We are elected into love.

Irene Claremont de Castillejo

*An old man in love is like
a flower in winter.*

PORTUGUESE PROVERB

*O, tell her, brief is life
but love is long.*

*ALFRED, LORD
TENNYSON*

Who can give law to lovers? Love is a greater law to itself.

BOETHIUS

To love a woman who scorns you is to lick honey from a thorn.

WELSH PROVERB

I judge how much a man cares for a woman by the space he allots her under a jointly shared umbrella.

JIMMY CANNON

*The way to a man's heart
is through his stomach*

PROVERB

*Remember
the old saying, "Faint heart
ne'er won fair lady."*

MIGUEL DE CERVANTES

This being in love is great—
you get a lot of compliments
and begin to think you
are a great guy.

F. SCOTT FITZGERALD

Falling in love is not an extension of one's limits or boundaries; it is a partial and temporary collapse of them

M. SCOTT PECK

*Love that stammers,
that stutters, is apt to be the
love that loves best.*

GABRIELA MISTRAL

*B*revity may be the soul of wit,
but not when someone's saying "I love you."
When someone's saying "I love you,"
he always ought to give a lot of details: Like, why
does he love you? And, how much does he love
you? And, when and where did he first begin to
love you? Favorable comparisons with all the other
women he ever loved are also welcome. And even
though he insists it would take forever to count the
ways in which he loves you, let him start counting.

Judith Viorst

*Love is never without
jealousy.*

JAMES KELLY

If you wish,
I shall grow irreproachably
tender:
Not a man, but a cloud
in trousers!

VLADIMIR MAYAKOVSKI

*H*elen, thy beauty is to me

Like those Nicean barks of yore,

That gently, o'er a perfumed sea,

The weary, wayworn wanderer bore

To his own native shore.

Edgar Allan Poe

*Speak, cousin, or,
if you cannot, stop his mouth
with a kiss.*

— WILLIAM SHAKESPEARE

*I like not only to be loved,
but to be told I am loved.*

GEORGE ELIOT

*One of the
best things about love is
just recognizing a man's step
when he climbs the stairs.*

COLETTE

*Thou art to me
a delicious torment.*

~

R ALPH W ALDO E MERSON

It is difficult to know
at what moment love begins;
it is less difficult to know
that it has begun.

HENRY WADSWORTH
LONGFELLOW

Love is like the measles —
all the worse when it comes
late in life.

DOUGLAS JERROLD

What is a kiss?
Why this, as some approve:
The sure, sweet cement, glue,
and lime of love.

ROBERT HERRICK

*Desire is the
very essence of man.*

~

BENEDICT SPINOZA

Love doesn't drop on you unexpectedly; you have to give off signals, sort of like an amateur radio operator.

HELEN GURLEY BROWN

I arise from dreams of thee
In the first sweet sleep of night,
When the winds are breathing low,
And the stars are shining bright.

Percy Bysshe Shelley

Love is the fire of life;
it either consumes or purifies.

~

ANONYMOUS

48

The magic of first love is our ignorance that it can ever end.

BENJAMIN DISRAELI

A lovely trick designed by nature to stop speech when words become superfluous.

INGRID BERGMAN
(on kissing)

*The heart has its reasons
which reason knows nothing of.*

~

BLAISE PASCAL

How do I love thee?

Let me count the ways.

I love thee to the depth

and breadth and height

My soul can reach . . .

Elizabeth Barrett Browning

*I*t took great courage to ask a

beautiful young woman to marry me.

Believe me, it is easier to play the whole

of *Petrushka* on the piano.

Arthur Rubinstein

*L*ove to faults is always blind,

Always is to joy inclined,

Lawless, winged, and unconfined,

And breaks all chains from every mind.

~ *William Blake* ~

Send two dozen roses to Room 424 and put 'Emily, I love you' on the back of the bill.

GROUCHO MARX

Our love is so furious that we burn each other out.

RICHARD BURTON
(after his second divorce from
Elizabeth Taylor)

The meeting of two
personalities is like the contact
of two chemical substances:
if there is any reaction,
both are transformed.

CARL JUNG

A man in love mistakes a harelip for a dimple.

JAPANESE PROVERB

*T*wo such as you

with such a master speed

Cannot be parted nor be swept away

From one another once you are agreed

That life is only life forevermore

Together wing to wing and oar to oar.

Robert Frost

(inscribed on gravestone of Frost
and his wife, Elinor)

*L*ove makes up for the lack of

long memories by a sort of magic.

All other affections need a past: love

creates a past which envelops us,

as if by enchantment.

Benjamin Constant

But there's nothing half so sweet in life
As love's young dream.

❧

THOMAS MOORE

My most brilliant achievement was my ability to be able to persuade my wife to marry me.

WINSTON CHURCHILL

Old love rusts not.

GERMAN PROVERB

*Love is blind —
but not the neighbors.*

MEXICAN PROVERB

*L*et us go then,
you and I,
When the evening is spread out

against the sky

Like a patient etherized upon a table.

 T. S. Eliot

*No matter
what the subject,
the subject is
always love.*

INGRID BENGIS

*L*ove is such a funny thing;

It's very like a lizard;

It twines itself around your heart

And penetrates your gizzard.

Anonymous

Love, like fortune,
turns upon a wheel, and
is very much given to
rising and falling.

SIR JOHN VANBRUGH

Those who love deeply never grow old; they may die of old age, but they die young.

Sir Arthur Wing Pinero

Love lives in cottages
as well as in courts.

ENGLISH PROVERB

*I*t was a very spasmodic courtship, conducted mainly at long distance with a great clanking of coins in dozens of phone booths.

Jacqueline Kennedy

How many loved

your moments of glad grace,

And loved your beauty with love false or true;

But one man loved the pilgrim soul in you,

And loved the sorrows of your changing face.

William Butler Yeats

No love like the first love.

PROVERB

*To be able to say how much
you love is to love but little.*

PETRARCH

*How sad and bad and
mad it was —
But then, how it was sweet!*

ROBERT BROWNING

Hell, Madame,
is to love no longer.

***

George S. Bernanos

*Take away leisure and
Cupid's bow is broken.*

OVID

*There are three things
that can never be hidden —
love, a mountain, and one
riding on a camel.*

ARAB PROVERB

*O*lympia Dukakis:

Do you love him, Loretta?

Cher: No.

Olympia Dukakis: Good.

When you love 'em, they drive you crazy,

'cause they know they can.

 *Moonstruck*

I was in love with the whole world and all that lived in its rainy arms.

LOUISE ERDRICH

*Love is like an hourglass,
with the heart filling up as the
brain empties.*

❧

JULES RENARD

A lover's eyes will gaze an eagle blind.

WILLIAM SHAKESPEARE

*I*f love were what the rose is,

And I were like the leaf,

Our lives would grow together

In sad or singing weather.

Algernon Charles
Swinburne

The attraction of one creature
for another, even when condemned by
reason for its passionate origin, is always
worthy of respect, because it reveals to
us something of the order of creation.

 *A. Carré*

In the spring a young man's fancy lightly turns to thoughts of love.

ALFRED, LORD TENNYSON

You see I thought love got easier over the years so it didn't hurt so bad when it hurt, or feel so good when it felt good. I thought it smoothed out and old people hardly noticed it. I thought it curled up and died, I guess. Now I saw it rear up like a whip and lash.

 Louise Erdrich

*For news of the heart
ask the face.*

GUINEAN PROVERB

I feel again a spark of that ancient flame.

VIRGIL

We are all born for love; it is the principle of existence and its only end.

BENJAMIN DISRAELI

*In the human heart,
love is the torrid zone.*

*Jacques-Henri
Bernardin
De Saint-Pierre*

*There is no remedy for love
but to love more.*

HENRY DAVID THOREAU

With all thy faults
I love thee still.

WILLIAM COWPER

To be in love with someone who doesn't love back gives you a pain in the chest at night.

BENNY HILL

They gave each other
a smile with a future in it.

RING LARDNER

*T*ime

is

Too slow for those who wait,

Too swift for those who fear,

Too long for those who grieve,

Too short for those who rejoice,

But for those who love, time is

Eternity. Hours fly, Flowers die,

New days, New ways, Pass by.

Love stays.

Anonymous

(inscription on a sundial at the University of Virginia)

Love is ... the universal thirst for a communion not merely of the senses, but of our whole nature.

PERCY BYSSHE SHELLEY

*U*nremembered and afar
I watched you as I watched a star,
Through darkness struggling into view,
And loved you better than you knew.

Elizabeth Akers Allen

*We discovered in each other
and ourselves worlds, galaxies,
a universe.*

~

ANNE RIVERS SIDDONS

If it is your time love will
track you down like a cruise missile.
If you say "No! I don't want it right
now," that's when you'll get it for sure.
Love will make a way out of no way.
Love is an exploding cigar which
we willingly smoke.

Lynda Barry

Lovers are madmen.

PROVERB

How much better
is thy love than wine!

SONG OF SOLOMON 4:10

Love is like measles:
you can get it only once,
and the later in life it occurs
the tougher it goes.

H. W. SHAW
(Josh Billings)

*Don't threaten me
with love, baby.*

❧

BILLIE HOLIDAY

Whoso loves believes
the impossible.

ELIZABETH BARRETT
BROWNING

The pains of love
be sweeter far
Than all other pleasures are.

*J*OHN *D*RYDEN

Nicolas Cage:
I'm in love with you.
Cher:
Snap out of it!

Moonstruck

*L*ove," she said, "seems to pump me full of vitamins. It makes me feel as if the *sun were shining* and my hat was right and my shoes were right and my frock was right and my stockings were right, and somebody had just left me ten thousand a year."

P. G. Wodehouse

Shall I compare thee to a
summer's day?
Thou art more lovely and
more temperate...

WILLIAM SHAKESPEARE

Love: A season's pass on the shuttle between heaven and hell.

DON DICKERMAN

Come live with me,

and be my love,

And we will some new pleasures prove

Of golden sands, and crystal brooks,

With silken lines, and silver hooks.

 *John Donne*

$\mathcal{T}$here is only one situation I can think of in which men and women make an effort to read better than they usually do. [It is] when they are in love and reading a love letter.

~ *Mortimer Adler* ~

*At the touch of love
every one becomes a poet.*

PLATO

Love me in full being.

~

ELIZABETH BARRETT
BROWNING

Love is a symbol of eternity.
It wipes out all sense of time,
destroying all memory of a beginning
and all fear of an end.

Madame de Staël

*Two souls with but a
single thought,
Two hearts that beat as one.*

FRIEDRICH HALM

Their correspondence was something like a duet between a tuba and a piccolo.

DAVID HERBERT
DONALD
(on love letters of Thomas Wolfe
and Aline Bernstein)

*I just want you to love me,
primal doubts and all.*

WILLIAM HOLDEN
(as Max Schumacher in *Network*)

*It is astonishing
how little one feels poverty
when one loves.*

JOHN BULWER

*Unlove's the heavenless hell
and homeless home . . .
lovers alone wear sunlight.*

E. E. CUMMINGS

scape me?

Never—

Beloved!

While I am I, and you are you.

Robert Browning

*Love is a spendthrift,
leaves its arithmetic at home, is
always 'in the red.'*

PAUL SCHERER

I'd be crazy to propose to her, but when I see that profile of hers I feel the only thing worth doing in the world is to grab her and start shouting for clergymen and bridesmaids to come running.

P. G. Wodehouse

I have found it impossible to carry the heavy burden of responsibility and to discharge my duties as king as I would wish to do without the help and support of the woman I love.

Edward, duke of Windsor

Age does not protect you from love. But love, to some extent, protects you from age.

JEANNE MOREAU

*Love has never been a
question of age.
I shall never be so old as
to forget what love is.*

COLETTE

The heart can do anything.

Molière

*D*rink to me only with thine eyes,

And I will pledge with mine;

Or leave a kiss but in the cup,

And I'll not look for wine.

Ben Jonson

Love . . . is a quicksilver word;
though you see plainly where it is,
you have only to put your finger
on it to find that it is not there
but someplace else.

Morton Hunt

Absence diminishes mediocre passions and increases great ones, as the wind blows out candles and fans fire.

DUC DE LA ROCHEFOUCAULD

It's curious how, when you're in love, you yearn to go about doing acts of kindness to everybody.

P. G. WODEHOUSE

Humphrey Bogart:

If that plane leaves the ground

and you're not with him, you'll regret it—

maybe not today, maybe not tomorrow,

but soon, and for the rest of your life.

Ingrid Bergman: But what about us?

Humphrey Bogart: We'll always have Paris.

Casablanca

When you really want love you will find it waiting for you.

OSCAR WILDE

*Nothing spoils the
taste of peanut butter like
unrequited love.*

CHARLIE BROWN

She walks in beauty,

like the night

Of cloudless climes and starry skies;

And all that's best of dark and bright

Meet in her aspect and her eyes.

Lord Byron

One is very crazy
when in love.

FREUD

*Love, and a cough,
cannot be hid.*

❧

GEORGE HERBERT

Love

is the heart's immortal thirst
to be completely known
and all forgiven.

HENRY VAN DYKE

*L*ove is the magician, the enchanter,

that changes worthless things to joy, and makes

right royal kings and queens of common clay. It

is the *perfume of that wondrous flower,*

the heart, and without that sacred passion,

that divine swoon, we are less than beasts;

but with it, earth is heaven, and we are gods.

Robert G. Ingersoll

Who says pull never gets you anywhere? If love tugs at your heartstrings, you're sitting on top of the world.

BURTON HILLIS

The woman one loves always smells good.

REMY DE GOURMONT

Absence makes the heart grow fonder.

SEXTUS PROPERTIUS

Part II: True Love

True love does not consist
in gazing at each other,
but in looking together in
the same direction.

Antoine De
Saint-Exupéry

To live is to love.

~

LUDWIG BOERNE

One of the oldest human needs is having someone to wonder where you are when you don't come home at night.

MARGARET MEAD

Love is the life of man.

EMANUEL SWEDENBORG

*Never change when love
has found its home.*

SEXTUS PROPERTIUS

Beware of all the
paradoxical in love.
It is simplicity which saves,
it is simplicity which
brings happiness. . . .
Love should be love.

Charles Baudelaire

I know some good marriages—
marriages where both people
are just trying to get through their days
by helping each other,
being good to each other.

Erica Jong

*I have lived long enough
to know that the evening glow
of love has its own riches
and splendour.*

BENJAMIN DISRAELI

The sum which two married people owe to one another defies calculation. It is an infinite debt, which can only be discharged through all eternity.

Johann Wolfgang von Goethe

*Love is the part of us
that is real.*

GERALD JAMPOLSKY

There is a land of the living and a land of the dead and the bridge is love, the only survival, the only meaning.

THORNTON WILDER

*Love is staying awake
all night with a sick child,
or a very healthy adult.*

DAVID FROST

Love sought is good,
but given unsought is better.

———

WILLIAM SHAKESPEARE

A simple enough pleasure,
surely, to have breakfast alone with
one's husband, but how seldom married
people in the midst of life achieve it.

*Anne Morrow
Lindbergh*

*L*ove is patient and kind; love is not jealous or boastful; it is not arrogant or rude. Love does not insist on its own way; it is not irritable or resentful; it does not rejoice at wrong, but rejoices in the right. Love bears all things, believes all things, hopes all things, endures all things.

1 Corinthians 13:4–7

Love is the only service that power cannot command and money cannot buy.

ANONYMOUS

*Nothing is impossible
to a willing heart.*

JOHN HEYWOOD

*Nobody has ever
measured, not even poets,
how much the heart
can hold.*

ZELDA FITZGERALD

*A new broom sweeps
clean, but an old broom
knows the corners.*

**Virgin Island
Proverb**

*When you send
out real love, real love will
return to you.*

FLORENCE SCOVEL
SHINN

Life in common among people who love each other is the ideal of happiness.

GEORGE SAND

You must get your living by loving.

HENRY DAVID THOREAU

*W*hen you lay dying,
what it's about is the intimacy you've
known, *the touch of another
human being*. Ultimately, what
makes your life worthwhile are the
other people you've cared about.

~ *Sherry Lansing* ~

*A successful marriage
is an edifice that must be
rebuilt every day.*

❧

ANDRÉ MAUROIS

There is no more lovely, friendly and charming relationship, communion or company than a good marriage.

MARTIN LUTHER

How terrible when people are led to believe, or left to believe, that once they are in love they have nothing to do but live happily ever after, they have nothing further to learn.

~ Gerald Vann ~

Love is a tender plant;
when properly nourished, it
becomes sturdy and enduring,
but neglected it will soon
wither and die.

HUGH B. BROWN

*To love and be loved is to feel
the sun from both sides.*

DAVID VISCOTT

Nothing in love can be premeditated; it is as a power divine, that thinks and feels within us, unswayed by our control.

MADAME DE STAËL

Only the really plain people know about love — the very fascinating ones try so hard to create an impression that they soon exhaust their talents.

KATHARINE HEPBURN

When one loves somebody,
everything is clear—*where to go,*
what to do—it all takes care of itself
and one doesn't have to ask anybody
about anything.

 *Maxim Gorky*

The giving of love is an education in itself.

ELEANOR ROOSEVELT

The supreme happiness
of life is the conviction that
we are loved.

VICTOR HUGO

Real love is a permanently self-enlarging experience. Falling in love is not.

M. SCOTT PECK

The more I wonder...
the more I love.

~

ALICE WALKER

There is no fear
in love; but perfect love
casteth out fear.

I John 4:18

Love is or it ain't.
Thin love ain't love at all.

TONI MORRISON

*A good marriage is that
in which each appoints the other
guardian of his solitude.*

❧

RAINER MARIA RILKE

The Eskimo has fifty-two names for snow because it is important to them; there ought to be as many for love.

MARGARET ATWOOD

The loving are the daring.

BAYARD TAYLOR

[*My* wife] told me
one of the sweetest things one could
hear—"I am not jealous. But I am truly
sad for all the actresses who embrace you
and kiss you while acting, for with
them, you are only pretending."

Joseph Cotten

*It was enough just to sit
there without words.*

LOUISE ERDRICH

Love is more pleasant once you get out of your twenties. It doesn't hurt all the time.

ANDREW A. ROONEY

Many waters cannot quench love, neither can the floods drown it.

SONG OF SOLOMON 8:7

Love has nothing to do with what you are expecting to get—only with what you are expecting to give—which is everything.

KATHARINE HEPBURN

Love cures people, the ones who receive love and the ones who give it, too.

KARL A. MENNINGER

Love comforteth like sunshine after rain.

WILLIAM SHAKESPEARE

No love, no friendship can cross the path of our destiny without leaving some mark on it forever.

François Mauriac

Grief can take care of itself, but to get the full value from joy you must have somebody to divide it with.

MARK TWAIN

Two persons who love each other are in a place more holy than the interior of a church.

WILLIAM PHELPS

Love is an attempt to change a piece of a dream world into reality.

THEODOR REIK

A life without love is like a year without summer.

SWEDISH PROVERB

From success you get a lot of things, but not that great inside thing that love brings you.

SAM GOLDWYN

To love I must have
something I can put my
arms around.

HENRY WARD BEECHER

In love there are no vacations. No such thing. Love has to be lived fully with its boredom and all that.

MARGUERITE DURAS

*Perhaps the chief business
of life is simply to learn how
to love.*

⌣

MARSHA SINETAR

In our life there is a single color, as on an artist's palette, which provides the meaning of life and art. It is the color of love.

Marc Chagall

*Rigidity is prevented
most of the time as love and
compassion mesh us into
tolerant human beings.*

KAETHE S. CRAWFORD

*The entire sum of
existence is the magic of being
needed by just one person.*

Vi Putnam

The first duty of love
is to listen.

PAUL TILLICH

*Familiar acts
are beautiful through love.*

PERCY BYSSHE SHELLEY

Love cannot be forced,
love cannot be coaxed or
teased. It comes out of
Heaven, unasked, unsought.

PEARL S. BUCK

*O*n the day when it will be possible for woman to love not in her weakness but in her strength, not to escape herself but to find herself, not to abase herself but to assert herself— on that day love will become for her, as for man, a source of life and not of mortal danger.

Simone de Beauvoir

All, everything that I understand, I understand only because I love.

LEO TOLSTOY

*L*ove is indeed not a state that

we are "in" or "out" of.

It comes as a gift when we risk ourselves,

our *whole* selves. . . .

 *Penelope Washbourn*

[*Love is*]
friendship set on fire.

JEREMY TAYLOR

At the end of what is called the
'sexual life' the only love which has lasted is
the love which has everything, every
disappointment, every failure and every
betrayal, which has accepted even the sad fact
that in the end there is no desire so deep as
the simple desire for companionship.

Graham Greene

*L*ove between two people is such a precious thing. It is not a possession. I no longer need to possess to complete myself. True love becomes my freedom.

Angela
L. Wozniak

*True love comes quietly,
without banners or flashing
lights. If you hear bells,
get your ears checked.*

~

ERICH SEGAL

*T*he strongest influences in my life
and my work are always whomever
I love. Whomever I love and am with
most of the time, or whomever
I *remember* most vividly.

Tennessee Williams

*Absence sharpens love,
presence strengthens it.*

THOMAS FULLER

Friendship, which is of its nature
a delicate thing, fastidious, slow of
growth, is easily checked, will hesitate,
demur, recoil where love, good old
blustering love, bowls ahead and
blunders through every obstacle.

 Colette

*To love deeply
in one direction makes us
more loving in all others.*

ANNE SWETCHINE

Grumbling
is the death of love.

———

MARLENE DIETRICH

Love consists in this,
that two solitudes protect and
touch and greet each other.

RAINER MARIA RILKE

Loving, like prayer,
is a power as well
as a process. It's curative.
It is creative.

ZONA GALE

We cannot really love
anybody with whom
we never laugh.

Agnes Replier

What is yours is mine,
and all mine is yours.

*P*LAUTUS

One advantage of marriage, it seems
to me, is that when you fall out of love
with him, or he falls out of love with
you, it keeps you together until
you maybe fall in love again.

Judith Viorst

Husband and wife in perfect concord are like the music of the harp and lute.

CHINESE PROVERB

*I*t is a lovely thing to have
a husband and wife developing together and
having the feeling of falling in love again.
That is what marriage really means:
helping one another to reach
the full status of being persons,
responsible and autonomous beings
who do not run away from life.

Paul Tournier

Love is a choice—not simply,
or necessarily, a rational choice,
but rather a willingness
to be present to others without
pretense or guile.

— *Carter Heyward* —

*L*ove is a flame which burns in heaven, and whose soft reflections radiate to us. Two worlds are opened, two lives given to it. It is by love that we double our being; it is by love that we approach God.

~ *Aimee Martin* ~

Love keeps the cold out better than a cloak. It serves for food and raiment.

HENRY WADSWORTH
LONGFELLOW

Tell me whom you love,
and I'll tell you
who you are.

❧

AFRICAN-AMERICAN
PROVERB

Love, you know,
seeks to make happy
rather than to be happy.

RALPH CONNOR

The one thing that I know about love for sure is that it's the only game in town and that you must keep going back to bat again and again and again. I have no respect for anyone who says they've given up, or that they're not looking or that they're tired. That is to abrogate one's responsibility as a human being.

Harlan Ellison

The pleasures and the cares of
ambitious goals attained, even with
boundless power, are nothing beside the
intimate happiness to be found
in affection and in love.

 *Stendhal*

The world has grown suspicious of anything that looks like a happy married life.

OSCAR WILDE

*When husband and wife
live in harmony,
they can dry up the ocean
without a bucket.*

VIETNAMESE PROVERB

*Marriage is the deep,
deep peace of the double bed
after the hurly-burly
of the chaise lounge.*

MRS. PATRICK CAMPBELL

This is one of the miracles
of love: it gives . . . a power of seeing
through its own enchantments and
yet not being disenchanted.

C. S. Lewis

Grow old along with me!
The best is yet to be,
The last of life, for which
the first was made . . .

ROBERT BROWNING

*One's best asset
is a sympathetic spouse.*

EURIPIDES

There is no surprise more magical than the surprise of being loved: it is God's finger on man's shoulder.

CHARLES MORGAN

*Married couples
who love each other tell
each other a thousand things
without talking.*

CHINESE PROVERB

*L*ove is just love, or love *is;*

the concept of "divine" or "human"

doesn't make any difference to love.

For love does not discriminate;

it only unites and unifies
everything.

~ *Dhiravamsa* ~

Cultivate
a heart of love that
knows no anger.

CAMBODIAN PROVERB

*Love is an energy
which exists of itself.
It is its own value.*

THORNTON WILDER

Love is what you've been through with somebody.

~

JAMES THURBER

(quoting a married women with six children)

The moment we exercise
our affections, the earth is
metamorphosed; there is no winter,
and no night; all tragedies,
all ennuis vanish—all furies even.

Ralph Waldo Emerson

*True love is like ghosts,
which everybody talks about
and few have seen.*

DUC DE
LA ROCHEFOUCAULD

*H*appiness comes more from loving
than being loved; and often when our affection
seems wounded it is only our vanity bleeding.
To love, and to be hurt often,
and to love again—this is
the brave and happy life.

J. E. Buckrose

*Love is, above all,
the gift of oneself.*

JEAN ANOUILH

The love we have in our youth
is superficial compared
to the love that an old man
has for his old wife.

WILL DURANT

Nothing matters but [love]. It demolishes the days and happily turns them into passageways.

GRETEL EHRLICH

*Love can do all
but raise the Dead.*

EMILY DICKINSON

Love is not blind
—it sees more, not less.
But because it sees more,
it is willing to see less.

RABBI JULIUS GORDON

*Take away love and
our earth is a tomb.*

ROBERT BROWNING

*Where there is great love
there are always miracles.*

WILLA CATHER

*A*mericans, who make more of marrying for love than any other people, also break up more of their marriages, but the figure reflects not so much the failure of love as the determination of people not to live without it.

Morton Hunt

It is a curious thought,
but it is only when you see people
looking ridiculous, that you realize just
how much you love them.

— *Agatha Christie* —

*There is only one
happiness in life,
to love and be loved.*

GEORGE SAND

Love doesn't just sit there
like a stone; it has to be
made, like bread, remade
all the time, made new.

Ursula K. Le Guin

*E*veryone has experienced that truth: that love, like a running brook, is disregarded, taken for granted; but when the brook freezes over, then people begin to remember how it was when it ran, and they want it to run again.

 *Kahlil Gibran*

Don't be afraid to feel as angry or as loving as you can.

❧

LENA HORNE

Love involves a peculiar unfathomable combination of understanding and misunderstanding.

DIANE ARBUS

*L*ove cannot accept what it is.
Everywhere on earth it cries out against
kindness, compassion, intelligence,
everything that leads to compromise.
Love demands the impossible, the absolute,
the sky on fire, inexhaustible springtime,
life after death, and death itself
transfigured into eternal life.

Albert Camus

*Love doesn't make
the world go 'round.
Love is what makes the
ride worthwhile.*

FRANKLIN P. JONES

*While faith makes all
things possible, it is love that
makes all things easy.*

~

EVAN H. HOPKINS

The story of love is not important.

What is important is that

one is capable of love.

It is perhaps the only glimpse we

are permitted of eternity.

 *Helen Hayes*

*Y*ou will reciprocally promise love,
loyalty and matrimonial honesty.
We only want for you this day that these words
constitute the principle of your entire life
and that with the help of divine grace
you will observe these solemn vows
that today, before God,
you formulate.

Pope John Paul II
(solemnizing a marriage)

*We have all known
the long loneliness and
we have learned that the
only solution is love.*

DOROTHY DAY

*A*y me! for aught that
I could ever read,
Could ever hear by tale or history,
The course of true love never
did run smooth.

William Shakespeare

I would like to have engraved
inside every wedding band
Be kind to one another.
This is the Golden Rule of marriage and
the secret of making love last
through the years.

Randolph Ray

Love opens the doors
into everything, as far as I can see,
including and perhaps most of all,
the door into one's own secret,
and often terrible and
frightening, real self.

May Sarton

*One leg
cannot dance alone.*

***

EAST AFRICAN PROVERB

*L*ove is that vital essence that pervades

and permeates, from the center to the

circumference, the graduating circles

of all thought and action.

Love is the talisman of human weal and woe

—the open sesame to every soul.

Elizabeth Cady Stanton

*To love is
to receive
a glimpse of heaven.*

KAREN SUNDE

Love is not weakness.
It is strong.
Only the sacrament of
marriage can contain it.

BORIS PASTERNAK

[*Love is*]
the ultimate expression
of the will to live.

~

THOMAS WOLFE

Love demands all,
and has a right to all.

LUDWIG VAN BEETHOVEN

You can depend
so much on certain people,
you can set your watch by them.
And that's love, even if it
doesn't seem very exciting.

Sylvester Stallone

*Let there be spaces
in your togetherness.*

KAHLIL GIBRAN

*Love comes gradually
with our worry, relief, and
care —with what we have
invested of ourselves.*

FRANCES KARLEN
SANTAMARIA

He was comforted by one of
the simpler emotions which some human
beings are lucky enough to experience.
He knew when he died he would be
watched by someone he loved.

Noel Annan

(on E. M. Forster)

*T*rouble is a part of your life,
and if you don't share it, you don't give
the person who loves you enough chance
to love you enough.

～ *Dinah Shore* ～

Love is immortality
struggling within
a mortal frame.

A. VICTOR MURRAY

*He who finds not love
finds nothing.*

SPANISH PROVERB

*The love we give away
is the only love we keep.*

ELBERT HUBBARD

*It is better not to live
than not to love.*

HENRY DRUMMOND

*There is always
something left to love.
And if you ain't learned that,
you ain't learned nothing.*

LORRAINE HANSBERRY

That Love is all there is,
Is all we know of Love;
It is enough, the freight should be
Proportioned to the groove.

 Emily Dickinson

*A successful marriage
requires falling in love
many times, always with
the same person.*

MIGNON McLAUGHLIN

*Y*ou can see them alongside the

shuffleboard courts in Florida or on

the porches of the old folks'

homes up north . . . They are in love,

they have always been in love,

although sometimes they would have denied it.

Ernest Havemann

PART III: FAMILIAL AND BROTHERLY LOVE

There can be no situation in life in which
the conversation of my dear sister will not
administer some comfort to me.

Lady Mary Wortley Montagu

The most important thing a father can do for his children is to love their mother.

THEODORE HESBURGH

*R*omance fails us and so
do friendships, but the relationship of
parent and child, less noisy than all
others, remains *indelible* and
indestructible, the strongest
relationship on earth.

~ *Theodor Reik* ~

When you look at your life,
the greatest happinesses
are family happinesses.

~

Dr. Joyce Brothers

Who ran to help me when I fell,

And would some pretty story tell,

Or kiss the place to make it well?

My Mother.

Anne Taylor

You feel so much love for your first child that you wonder how you could possibly love the second one as much. Then you discover how infinite your capacity to love is.

— Linda D'Agrosa —

*Here all mankind
is equal: rich and poor alike,
they love their children.*

EURIPIDES

*L*ove makes people look
at the bright side of things.
They do see the bad things, but they
make a great effort to see the good,
so they do see the good.

Anonymous

*Love is all we have,
the only way that each can
help the other.*

EURIPIDES

That best portion of

a good man's life,

His little, nameless, unremembered acts

Of kindness and of love.

William Wordsworth

Be kindly affectioned one to another with brotherly love.

ROMANS 12:10

Love is the life of the soul.
It is the harmony
of the universe.

WILLIAM ELLERY
CHANNING

$\mathcal{I}$ have learned that to have

a good friend is the purest of all

God's gifts, for it is a love that

has no exchange of payment.

Frances Farmer

Love is the doorway through
which the human soul passes from
selfishness to service
and from solitude to kinship
with all mankind.

Anonymous

*Thou shalt love
thy neighbor as thyself.*

LEVITICUS 19:18

You don't raise heroes, you raise sons. And if you treat them like sons, they'll turn out to be heroes, even if it's just in your own eyes.

Walter M. Schirra, Sr.

*G*od sent children for another purpose
than merely to keep up the race—to enlarge
our hearts; and to make us unselfish and
full of kindly sympathies and affections;
to give our souls higher aims; to call out all our
faculties to extended enterprise and exertion;
and to bring round our firesides bright faces,
happy smiles, and loving, tender hearts.

～ ～ ～

Mary Botham Howitt

*Friendship
is love refined.*

❧

SUSANNAH CENTLIVRE

I just owe almost everything to
my father [and] it's passionately
interesting for me that the things that
I learned in a small town, in a very
modest home, are just the things that
I believe have won the election.

Margaret Thatcher

*A friend is one
who knows all about you
and likes you anyway.*

CHRISTI MARY WARNER

*A new commandment
I give unto you, that you
love one another.*

JOHN 13:34

Whenever you are
confronted with an opponent,
conquer him with love.

MOHANDAS GANDHI

*You don't choose
your family. They are
God's gift to you,
as you are to them.*

DESMOND TUTU

The baby is practicing loving for life.
The more he can love, now, and feel
himself loved back, the more generous
with, and *accepting* of, all kinds
of love he will be, right through his life.

~ *Penelope Leach* ~

*I do not love him because
he is good, but because
he is my little child.*

RABINDRANATH TAGORE

I love my daughter. She and I have shared my body. There is a part of her mind that is a part of mine. But when she was born, she sprang from me like a slippery fish, and has been swimming away ever since.

— *Amy Tan* —

*I*t seems to me that since I've had children, *I've grown richer and deeper.* They may have slowed down my writing for a while, but when I did write, I had more of a self to speak from.

— *Anne Tyler* —

*The mother's heart
is the child's schoolroom.*

HENRY WARD BEECHER

For me, motherhood has been

the one true, great, and

wholly successful romance.

It is the only love I have known that

is expansive and that could have

stretched to contain with equal passion

more than one object. . . .

Erma Kurtz

The best smell is bread,
the best savour salt,
the best love that of children.

PROVERB

*Love is the strongest force
the world possesses, and yet it
is the humblest imaginable.*

MOHANDAS GANDHI

It is a wonderful seasoning of all enjoyments to think of those we love.

MOLIÈRE

If you give your life as a wholehearted response to love, then love will wholeheartedly respond to you.

MARIANNE WILLIAMSON

A mother is not a person to lean on but a person to make leaning unnecessary.

DOROTHY CANFIELD FISHER

*L*ove is will, the will to share
your happiness with all.
Being happy—making happy—this
is the rhythm of love.

Nasaragada
Ha Maharaj

I love my mother,

not as a prisoner of atherosclerosis,

but as a person; and I must love her

enough to accept her as she is,

now, for as long as this

dwindling may take.

Madeleine L'Engle

*Love is the key
to the universe which
unlocks all doors.*

Anonymous

You will find as you look back
upon your life that the moments
when you have really lived are the
moments when you have done
things in the spirit of love.

Henry Drummond

To talk to a child,
to fascinate him, is much more difficult

than to win an electoral victory.

But it is also more rewarding.

COLETTE

One's life has value so long
as one attributes value to the life
of others, by means of love,
friendship, indignation
and compassion.

Simone de Beauvoir

*Old as she was,
she still missed her daddy
sometimes.*

— **GLORIA NAYLOR**

*C*ompared to other feelings,

love is an elemental cosmic force

weaving a disguise of meekness. . . .

It is not a state of mind;

it is the foundation

of the universe.

— *Boris Pasternak* —

The cure for all the ills and wrongs, the cares, the sorrows, and the crimes of humanity, all lie in that one word "love." It is the divine vitality that everywhere produces and restores life. To each and every one of us, it gives the power of working miracles if we will.

Lydia Maria Child

If we make our goal to live a life
of compassion and unconditional love,
then the world will indeed become
a garden where all kinds of flowers
can bloom and grow.

Elisabeth Kübler-Ross

I have listened to the realm
of the Spirit. I have heard my own soul's
voice, and I have remembered that
love is the complete and unifying
thread of existence.

 *Mary Casey*

If we all discovered that we had only five minutes left to say all that we wanted to say, every telephone booth would be occupied by people calling other people to tell them that they loved them.

Christopher Morley

$\mathscr{W}$ithin our family there was no such thing as a person who did not matter. Second cousins thrice removed mattered. We knew —and thriftily made use of—everybody's middle name. We knew who was buried where. We all mattered, and the dead most of all.

Shirley Abbott

Love is not the product of any particular religion. It is the rightful province of each and every human heart.

T. D. MUNDA

You have to love your children unselfishly. That's hard. But it's the only way.

BARBARA BUSH

Love has power that dispels Death; charm that conquers the enemy.

KAHLIL GIBRAN

Love those who love you.

VOLTAIRE

*W*ork is what gives us our bread
and butter, stability and place in the
world, *but love keeps us human.*
Any old kind of love.

~ Barbara Holland ~

*Love is the only force
capable of transforming an
enemy into a friend.*

~

MARTIN LUTHER
KING, JR.

*L*ove many things, for therein lies
the true strength, and whosoever loves
much performs much, and can
accomplish much, and what is
done in love is well done.

~ *Vincent van Gogh* ~

*Love is to the moral nature
exactly what the sun
is to the earth.*

HONORÉ DE BALZAC

Perfect love sometimes does not come until the first grandchild.

WELSH PROVERB

Never love unless you can
Bear with all the faults
of man.

THOMAS CAMPION

Nowadays we don't think much of a man's love for an animal; we laugh at people who are attached to cats. But if we stop loving animals, aren't we bound to stop loving humans too?

Alexander Solzhenitsyn

*Y*ou must love all that God has created,
both his entire world and each single tiny
sand grain of it. Love each tiny leaf, each
beam of sunshine. You must love the animals,
love every plant. If you love all things,
you will also attain the divine mystery that
is in all things. For then your ability to perceive
the truth will grow every day, and your mind
will open itself to an all-embracing love.

Fyodor Dostoyevsky

Loving a child doesn't mean giving in to all his whims; to love him is to bring out the best in him, to teach him to love what is difficult.

~ *Nadia Boulanger* ~

My mother is a poem
I'll never be able to write
though everything I write is
a poem to my mother.

SHARON DOUBIAGO

For there is no friend like a sister

In calm or stormy weather;

To cheer one on the tedious way,

To fetch one if one goes astray,

To lift one if one totters down,

To strengthen whilst one stands.

Christina Rossetti

Love is spiritual fire.

EMANUEL SWEDENBORG

Making the decision to have a child—it's momentous. It is to decide forever to have your heart go walking around outside your body.

— Elizabeth Stone —

The biggest surprise, which is also the best, is that I didn't know I would love motherhood as much as I do.

DEBORAH NORVILLE

*Friendship is one heart
in two bodies.*

JOSEPH ZABARA

Children need love,
especially when they
do not deserve it.

HAROLD S. HUBERT

Give a little love to a child,
and you get a great deal back.

JOHN RUSKIN

*Love, which is the essence
of God, is not for levity,
but for the total worth
of man.*

RALPH WALDO EMERSON

We must learn the loving of a first child step by step, as we learn to sustain love in marriage. The loving of a first baby is like an acquired gift, or skill. The second child, I imagine, comes into that love ready-made.

Frances Karlen Santamaria

It is not a matter of thinking a great deal but of loving a great deal, so do whatever arouses you most to love.

Saint Theresa of Avila

The theologian is right.
Why not admit it?
More than anything else
the world needs love.

SEBASTIAN DE GRAZIA

One's family is the most important thing in life. I look at it this way: one of these days I'll be over in a hospital somewhere with four walls around me. And the only people who'll be with me will be my family.

— Robert C. Byrd —

Flowers are lovely;
love is flower-like;
Friendship is a sheltering
tree.

SAMUEL TAYLOR COLERIDGE

*S*ome are kissing mothers and
some are scolding mothers, but it is love
just the same, and most mothers kiss and
scold together.

Pearl S. Buck

Mama!
Dearest mama!
I know you are my
one true friend.

NIKOLAI GOGOL

*Never forget that
the most powerful force
on earth is love.*

NELSON ROCKEFELLER

The happy man is he
who lives the life of love,
not for the honors it may
bring, but for the life itself.

R. J. BAUGHAN

*K*eep love in your heart.
A life without it is like a sunless
garden when the flowers are dead.
The consciousness of loving and being
loved brings a warmth and richness to
life that nothing else can bring.

Oscar Wilde

To love is to love the person. It is not to love the good or the perfect things to be found in that person.

~ *Georgette Butcher* ~

*A mother understands
what a child does not say.*

~

*J*ewish proverb

*You know full as well as
I do the value of sisters'
affections to each other; there
is nothing like it in this world.*

Charlotte Brontë

We can never know love if we try to
draw others to ourselves; nor can we find it
by centering our love in them. For love is
infinite; it is never ours to create.
We can only channel it from its source in
infinity to all whom we meet.

J. Donald Walter

Love is an act of endless forgiveness.

Peter Ustinov

The family is one of nature's masterpieces.

George Santayana

The text of this book was set in Centaur and Swanson

by Harry Chester Inc.

Cover and interior design

by Judith Stagnitto Abbate